Be An Expert!™

Kittens

Erin Kelly

Children's Press®
An imprint of Scholastic Inc.

Contents

Know the Names

Be an expert! Get to know the names of these kittens.

Siamese

They talk a lot!
They say "meow."

Zoom In

Find these parts in the big picture.

blue eyes

paw

tail

whiskers

Maine Coons

They grow big.
They are called gentle giants.

adult Maine coon

Purr-fect Your Knowledge

Q: How did the Maine coon cat get its name?

A: They come from the state of Maine. And some people think they look like raccoons!

Manx

Look at that!
They have no tails.

Expert Fact

These kittens have some dog-like **habits**. They love to play fetch. And some even bury their toys.

Ragdolls

They love people. They will follow you around the house!

Purr-fect Your Knowledge

Q: Were Ragdolls named after dolls?

A: Yes. They **flop** like a rag doll when you pick them up. And they are happy to be carried around.

adult Ragdoll

Bengals

They have markings like a leopard!
They are good hunters.

Zoom In

Find these parts in the big picture.

ear

chest

hind leg

markings

Turkish Vans

Most kittens don't like water.
But these love to swim!

Purr-fect Your Knowledge

Q: How can you tell when Turkish vans are **upset**?

A: Their pink noses turn red!

Scottish Folds

These kittens are sweet. They like a lot of **affection**.

Expert Fact

Scottish folds are born with ears that point up. Their ears may fold down in a few weeks.

Sphynxes

They don't shed.

They hardly have any fur!

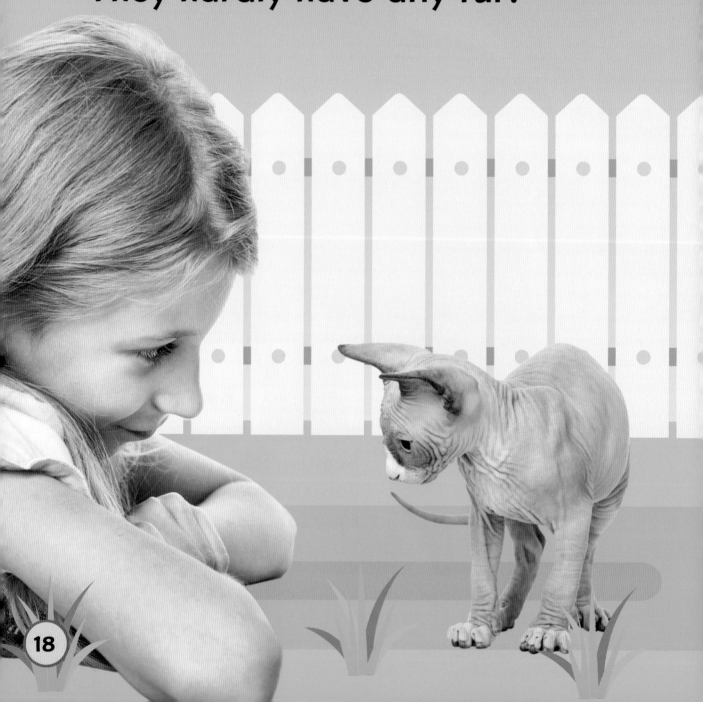

Purr-fect Your Knowledge

Q: How do you care for sphynxes?

A: Their skin gets oily. They need a bath every week.

19

All the Kittens

They are so cute.
Thanks, kittens!

1.

2.

5.

6.

Expert Quiz

Do you know the names of these kittens? Then you are an expert! See if someone else can name them too!

3.

4.

7.

8.

Answers: 1. Maine coons. 2. Siamese. 3. Bengal. 4. Scottish fold. 5. Turkish vans. 6. Sphynx. 7. Ragdoll. 8. Manx.

21

Meet an Expert

This is the owner of a cat café. Guests who come to the café to eat can also pet cats and play with them. What does she need to run her business?

She has **drinks**.

She has **cats**.

She has **menus**.

She has **cat food**.

Glossary

affection (uh-FEK-shuhn): love for someone or something familiar to you.

flop (FLAHP): to fall or drop heavily. This cat flops when you pick it up.

habits (HAB-its): activities or behaviors that are done regularly. Brushing your teeth is a good habit.

upset (uph-SET): to be nervous, sad, angry, or worried.

Index

Library of Congress Cataloging-in-Publication Data

Names: Kelly, Erin Suzanne, 1965- author.

Title: Kittens / Erin Kelly.

Description: New York: Scholastic Inc., 2021. | Series: Be an expert! | Includes index. | Audience: Ages 4-5. | Audience: Grades K-1. | Summary: "Book introduces the reader to kittens"—Provided by publisher.

Identifiers: LCCN 2020031765 | ISBN 9780531136737 (library binding) | ISBN 9780531136768 (paperback)

Subjects: LCSH: Kittens—Juvenile literature. | CYAC: Cats.

Classification: LCC SF445.7 .K45 2021 | DDC 636.8/07—dc23

LC record available at https://lccn.loc.gov/2020031765

Printed in Heshan, China 62

SCHOLASTIC, CHILDREN'S PRESS, BE AN EXPERT!™, and associated logos are trademarks and/or registered trademarks of Scholastic Inc.

1 2 3 4 5 6 7 8 9 10 R 30 29 28 27 26 25 24 23 22 21

Scholastic Inc., 557 Broadway, New York, NY 10012.

Art direction and design by THREE DOGS DESIGN LLC.

Photos © cover center: 101cats/Getty Images; cover center right: Sergey Ryumin/Getty Images; cover bottom left: Gandee Vasan/Getty Images; cover grass: almoond/Getty Images; 1 center left and throughout: Photodeti/Dreamstime; 2 top right: Anastasiia Prokofyeva/Dreamstime; 2 bottom left: 101cats/Getty Images; 2 bottom right: FLPA/Chris Brignell/age fotostock; 3 top right: Moredix/Dreamstime; 3 center left and throughout: Ozkan Bilgin/Anadolu Agency/Getty Images; 3 center right: RFcompany/age fotostock; 4 butterflies: posteriori/Getty Images; 5 bottom right: Okssi68/Dreamstime; 6-7 background: Alexei Sysoev/Dreamstime; 6 bottom: Anastasiia Prokofyeva/Dreamstime; 6 cat on bed right: Cynoclub/Dreamstime; 7 sidebar bottom: ultramarinfoto/Getty Images; 9 sidebar: Adogslifephoto/Dreamstime; 10 center: Moredix/Dreamstime; 10 bottom: Nature Picture Library/Alamy Images; 11 sidebar top: Cyndi Monaghan/Getty Images; 11 sidebar bottom: kali9/Getty Images; 11 center: Cyndi Monaghan/Getty Images; 12-13 foreground: Tanya Little/Getty Images; 12 bottom: Ian Mcglasham/Dreamstime; 14-15: Ozkan Bilgin/Anadolu Agency/Getty Images; 17 right: Juniors Bildarchiv/age fotostock; 19 bottom left: Chris Brignell/FLPA/age fotostock; 21 top: 101cats/Getty Images; 21 center right: Juniors Bildarchiv/age fotostock; 21 bottom left: petographer/Alamy Images; 22 menu: DNY59/Getty Images; 22 center: Leonhard Foeger/Reuters/Newscom; 23 top: Kamonrat Meunklad/EyeEm/Getty Images; 23 center top: Cyndi Monaghan/Getty Images.

All other photos © Shutterstock.